The seventy-six photographs of post offices featured on the inside front and back pages of *The Prairie Post Office* are the North Dakota post offices that were scheduled for closure in accord with the 2011 USPS Retail Access Optimization Initiative.

The Prairie Post Office

The Prairie Post Office

Enlarging the Common Life in Rural North Dakota

K. Amy Phillips & Steven R. Bolduc

Photographs by Wayne Gudmundson
History by Kevin Carvell

Foreword by Darryl Anderson

North Dakota State University Press
Dept. 2360, P.O. Box 6050, Fargo, ND 58108-6050
www.ndsu.edu/ahss/ndirs

North Dakota State University Press
Dept. 2360, P.O. Box 6050, Fargo, ND 58108-6050
www.ndsu.edu/ahss/ndirs

THE PRAIRIE POST OFFICE: ENLARGING THE COMMON LIFE IN RURAL NORTH DAKOTA
K. Amy Phillips and Steven R. Bolduc

©2017 by North Dakota State University Press
First Edition

ISBN: 978-0-911042-92-4
Library of Congress Control Number: 2016939824

Cover and interior design by Deb Tanner
Photographs by Wayne Gudmundson
Angela Beaton, Editorial Intern

Cover photo: Fingal, North Dakota

The publication of *The Prairie Post Office: Enlarging the Common Life in Rural North Dakota* is made possible by the generous support of donors to the NDSU Press Fund and the NDSU Press Endowment Fund.

The quotes used herein by individual former and current U.S. Postal Service® employees reflect the personal opinions and statements of the individuals quoted and are not meant in any way to reflect the views, statements or opinions of the U.S. Postal Service®.

U.S. Flag Stamp © United States Postal Service. All rights reserved. Used with permission.

For copyright permission, please contact Suzzanne Kelley at 701-231-6848 or suzzanne.kelley@ndsu.edu.

Printed in USA

Publisher's Cataloging-In-Publication Data
(Prepared by The Donohue Group, Inc.)

Names: Phillips, K. Amy, 1956– | Bolduc, Steven R., 1964– | Gudmundson, Wayne, photographer. | Carvell, Kevin, 1945– | Anderson, Darryl (Darryl J.), writer of supplementary textual content.
Title: The prairie post office : enlarging the common life in rural North Dakota / K. Amy Phillips & Steven R. Bolduc ; photographs by Wayne Gudmundson ; history by Kevin Carvell ; foreword by Darryl Anderson.
Description: First edition. | Fargo, ND : North Dakota State University Press, [2017] | Includes bibliographical references and index.
Identifiers: ISBN 978-0-911042-92-4
Subjects: LCSH: Post office stations and branches—North Dakota—History. | Rural free delivery—North Dakota—History.
Classification: LCC HE6376.A1 N67 2017 | DDC 383.49784—dc23

∞ This paper meets the requirements of ANSI/NISO Z39.48-1992
(Permanence of Paper).

The Prairie Post Office is dedicated to all former, current, and future United States Postal Service employees in rural North Dakota who not only ensure mail delivery but also, along with rural post office buildings, embody the message contained in the poem, "The Letter":

Messenger of sympathy and love

Servant of parted friends

Consoler of the lonely

Bond of the scattered family

Enlarger of the common life

Carrier of news and knowledge

Instrument of trade and industry

Promoter of mutual acquaintance

Of peace and of goodwill among men and nations

Note: "The Letter" was written by Dr. Charles W. Eliot, former president of Harvard University, and was slightly revised by President Woodrow Wilson. The poem above is the revised version, which is also inscribed on the outside of the former Washington, DC, Post Office, Massachusetts Avenue and North Capitol Street, now the site of the Smithsonian Institution's National Postal Museum.

Contents

Foreword

IN 2009, THEN POSTMASTER GENERAL Jack Potter described the universal delivery system of the US Postal Service as "one of our great national treasures." In their warm, rich, human, and valuable book, Professors Phillips and Bolduc have proven and illustrated the truth of that statement. And they have delivered that truth at a crucial turning point in the life of the Postal Service.

The authors have provided a concise and pointed summary of federal legislation that has damaged the viability and threatened the existence of rural postal services. As this book is approaching its completion, Congress is again considering legislation that may, or may not, preserve postal services for rural communities. In that context, the moving portraits presented here of intertwined lives of public servants and private citizens in rural communities carry an urgent message. The nature of rural community life in America turns in significant part on the role of the Postal Service in that life. It is impossible to separate rural communities and their postal services, for they are part of a single fabric. In communities so small that every person plays a known part, the role of the postmaster and of the letter carrier is central and critical.

In this richly illustrated history of the prairie post office, the authors have wisely used the candid and moving photographs of Wayne Gudmundson not simply to illustrate but literally to show the important presence of the Post Office in the local community. It is where the flag flies. It is a lifeline through which medicines, farm implements, materials as various as diamonds and baby chicks, wedding invitations, and love itself reach our rural communities. In a country where we idealize rural America, readers of this book must and will be moved and changed by the humanity of this story.

By telling this story, the authors inevitably have become advocates for the farmers, for small businesses, for the rural poor, and for rural communities, including tribal communities, that continue to rely heavily on postal services. As the authors observe, there is an irony to the calls made by some for the Postal Service to be operated more like a business or even to be privatized. In today's political climate, the call for privatization, which was famously uttered by Senator Barry Goldwater during his failed efforts to win the presidency, may be expected to re-emerge. To those calls, this book would seem to respond, "not so fast." The two great and efficient private carriers of parcels and urgent written messages, UPS and FedEx, the authors observe, rely on the US Postal Service to carry more than 25 percent of their parcels. The reason for that is very clear. It is not profitable to deliver a relatively small number of parcels to sparsely populated areas. That service can only be provided by the national treasure that is our universal postal network. That network is, as this book shows, one of the indispensable parts of our national infrastructure, along with our transportation networks and our other communications networks.

Legislation enacted in 2006 placed the Postal Service under enormous financial pressure to cut services of all kinds, including services to rural communities. By 2011, the Postal Service had responded with a plan to close or downsize more than 3,600 post offices, including 76 post offices in rural communities in North Dakota. That plan caused a backlash that saved most of those post offices but left them with substantially reduced hours of service. Sadly, the savings from those cuts are meager when compared to the cost to our rural communities. The League of Postmasters has pointed out that even if more than 3,600 post offices had been closed, the total savings from that effort would have been too small to help address the needs of the Postal Service.

For thirty-two years ending in 2013, I served as general counsel to the American Postal Workers Union, AFL-CIO, one of the two largest postal unions representing employees of the US Postal Service. In that capacity, I knew and helped negotiate with nine Postmasters General of the United States. I also represented the Union in proceedings before the Postal Rate Commission (after 2006, the Postal Regulatory Commission). Notably, the interests of postal employees often coincide with the in-terests of the rural communities described here. There is a tension between the legitimate need of large mailers to minimize their postage costs, which are multiplied by the millions of letters and parcels they send, and the interests of small businesses and individuals who live and work in communities that are sparsely populated and where it is less efficient to provide postal services. Large mailers, focused intently on their postage costs, have no interest in maintaining post offices in small communities that have insufficient volume to cover their costs.

The interest of postal employees in continuing to provide full postal services to all parts of the country coincides with the needs of our rural communities. This point is well illustrated by a struggle over postal rates in 2006. The Postal Service proposed a two-cent increase in the price of a First Class postage stamp. The Postal Workers Union presented testimony to the Postal Rate Commission showing that the price increase for a stamp could be held to one cent if large mailers were required to pay a small, marginally larger increase than the Postal Service had sought. The Commission ultimately recommended that course and the increase in the price of a stamp was held to one cent.

I also have been a close observer of the legislative process. For four years before I became counsel to the American Postal Workers Union, I served as counsel to the US Senate Committee on Labor and Human Resources. Because of the importance of federal legislation to the Postal Service and postal employees, I have continued to be concerned with postal legislation. And postal legislation is again pending in Congress as I write these words. There is a real possibility that Congress will enact legislation with problematic consequences for the

Postal Service and for the rural communities it serves. I hope that the important message in this moving book comes in time and reaches enough of the public officials who represent the people and places it depicts to ensure that these people and these places are protected.

Darryl Anderson
Former General Counsel of the American Postal Workers Union, AFL-CIO, and a founding principal of O'Donnell, Schwartz & Anderson, P.C.

Preface

THE UNITED STATES POSTAL SERVICE is a unique institution in American life. It contributed to the founding of the United States, reaches every household in the country, and provides a mechanism for personal communication and civic cohesion. Post office buildings often reflect the architecture and art of their times and serve as informal gathering places and symbols of community identity. Post offices are where parents go to pick up tax forms and where children go to send handmade notecards to distant grandparents. Like no other institution, the postal system is symbolic and concrete, personal and social, federal and local.

The US postal system has been the subject of scholarly examination, and we are indebted to Wayne Fuller whose *The American Mail: Enlarger of the Common Life* was an inspiration for the title of this book (and who himself was inspired by Charles W. Eliot's poem, reprinted here a few pages earlier). *The Prairie Post Office*, however, offers a new perspective since it focuses on the rural residents whose voices help to illuminate the valuable and varied roles of the post office in contemporary rural communities. *The Prairie Post Office* also offers a history chapter, ably written by Kevin Carvell, who scoured various resources and his own voluminous collection of North Dakota books to pull together a comprehensive and engaging narrative of mail service in northern Dakota Territory and the state of North Dakota.

Rural post offices have been under threat of closure in recent years, and rural residents have feared their loss. It is our intent that this book will provide a durable record of the services provided to prairie communities by post offices and their employees and that it will inform debates about the purpose and future of rural mail delivery by highlighting the central roles of rural postal employees in contributing to the present and future vitality of rural communities. Wayne Gudmundson's wonderful portraits of postal employees and postal customers reinforce the fact that people are at the heart of the postal system.

The Prairie Post Office is our tribute to the people in North Dakota and around the country who live and love a rural life and who understand, better than anyone, the institutions needed to support it.

K. Amy Phillips
Steven R. Bolduc
Fargo, North Dakota

Introduction

MOST OF US WHO ATTENDED elementary school in the United States may remember learning that Benjamin Franklin was the first Postmaster General of the United States. Franklin's mail system became the forerunner of today's United States Postal Service (USPS), but mail delivery stretches further back into the colonial period when the General Court of Massachusetts authorized official mail service in 1639 and designated the Boston home and tavern of Richard Fairbanks as an official repository for correspondence between Europe and the colonies.[1] During the colonial era and well after, many more taverns, inns, and homes doubled as post offices where local residents met to socialize and collect their mail. Post offices and mail delivery thus existed before, and contributed to, the founding of the United States. Stretching back more than three hundred years, the USPS is rich in history, personalities, and collective import for communities across the country.

The two of us, Steven R. Bolduc and K. Amy Phillips, who interviewed the individuals featured in this book, have memories of learning how to address and mail a letter, watching our parents talk with neighbors at the post office, and eagerly anticipating packages and correspondence via the postal service. We grew up admiring the impressive machinery, brass mailboxes, and the public art in the post office. The US flag outside the post office was a constant reminder that this building represented our connection to a larger whole.

Rural mail delivery is as important an institution to the development of rural United States as rural electrification, the Homestead Act, the land-grant university with its cooperative extension system, and the establishment of the United States Department of Agriculture. Contemporary changes in telecommunications and in demographic shifts between rural and urban spaces, however, have altered the patterns of use of postal services across the country.

When we heard about the USPS plan in 2011 to close seventy-six rural North Dakota post offices, our first thoughts were for the residents of those prairie communities. What would happen if they lost their post office? Where would they send or receive mail? How many postal employees in those towns might lose their jobs? In the context of these and other questions, a larger question emerged for us: What is the role of the post

---
[1] United States Postal Service (n.d.), *The United States Postal Service: An American History, 1775–2006*, Government Relations, United States Postal Service: Washington, DC.

office in rural North Dakota communities? We knew that the post office played an important communication role relative to mail service, but we wondered if there were additional roles of the post office and its employees that would, if lost, represent a more comprehensive blow to rural communities.

The US Post Office Department became the United States Postal Service under the Postal Reorganization Act of 1970 (PRA). Along with other changes, the PRA moved the postmaster general out of the president's Cabinet, started a postal career service that prohibited political appointments, and created an independent Postal Rate Commission. Under the PRA, postal employees gained collective bargaining rights due in large part to a federal postal workers wildcat strike in March 1970, motivated by low wages and poor working conditions.[2]

The PRA launched the USPS as an "independent establishment of the executive branch of the Government of the United States."[3] The new USPS was designed to operate less like a government department and more like a commercial enterprise, since Congress viewed the Post Office Department as able to use its postage, products, and services to pay its operating expenses.[4] Despite its corporate makeover, the official purpose of the USPS as articulated in Title 39, Section 101 of the US Code, did not change, and continues unchanged to the present:

(a) The United States Postal Service shall be operated as a basic and fundamental service provided to the people by the Government of the United States, authorized by the Constitution, created by Act of Congress, and supported by the people. The Postal Service shall have as its basic function the obligation to provide postal services to bind the Nation together through the personal, educational, literary, and business correspondence of the people. It shall provide prompt, reliable, and efficient services to patrons in all areas and shall render postal services to all communities. The costs of establishing and maintaining the Postal Service shall not be apportioned to impair the overall value of such service to the people.

(b) The Postal Service shall provide a maximum degree of effective and regular postal services to rural areas, communities, and small towns where post offices are not self-sustaining. No small post office shall be closed solely for operating at a deficit, it being the specific intent of the Congress that effective postal services be insured to residents of both urban and rural communities.[5]

On September 6, 2011, US Postmaster General Patrick Donahoe told a US Senate committee that the Postal Service was on the verge of bankruptcy, projecting a net loss of up to $10 billion by the end of the fiscal year. Do-

---

[2]D. Boyd & K. Chen (n.d.), "The History and Experiences of African Americans in America's Postal Service," Smithsonian National Postal Museum, http://postalmuseum.si.edu/AfricanAmericanhistory/p11.html.

[3]United States Postal Service (n.d.), About, "United States Postal Service," https://about.usps.com/publications/pub100/pub100_036.htm

[4]Office of the Inspector General (February 28, 2011), "A Study of the Risks and Consequences of the USPS OIG's Proposals to Change USPS's Funding of Retiree Benefits. Shifting Costs from USPS Ratepayers to Taxpayers." https://www.opm.gov/our-inspector-general/reports/2011/opm_oig_study_of_usps_oig_proposalsFeb282011.pdf

[5]United States Code 2013 Edition, Title 39 § 101, "Postal policy," https://www.gpo.gov/fdsys/pkg/USCODE-2013-title39/html/USCODE-2013-title39.

nahoe told the committee that "[t]he mailing industry, of which the Postal Service is only one component . . . makes up approximately seven percent of the country's Gross Domestic Product (GDP). Failure to act could be catastrophic."[6] Donahoe went on to say that the fiscal crisis was due to the drop in first-class mail revenue as a result of the growth of electronic communications and, more significantly, the burden of making an annual $5.5 billion payment to the Retiree Health Benefits pre-funding schedule. Under the 2006 Postal Accountability and Enhancement Act, the United States Postal Service, unlike any other public or private entity, was required to make the annual $5.5 billion retirement fund pre-payment over ten years, through 2016.[7]

Postmaster General Donahoe requested legislation that would provide the USPS with more flexibility in its business model, including changing the prefunding requirements, granting USPS the authority to determine delivery schedules, and allowing it to reduce its career, and unionized, workforce.[8] Simultaneous to this legislative initiative, the USPS had already begun a plan to close or downsize 3,652 postal retail facilities. This plan, called the Retail Access Optimization Initiative (RAOI), included an effort to replace traditional post offices with Village Post Offices—drugstores, grocery stores, self-service kiosks, etc.—that would sell postal products

and services.[9] Of the 3,652 postal facilities on the RAOI list, 76 were in the rural communities of North Dakota.[10]

The USPS employees and Congress (especially members from rural states) pushed back, and the Postal Regulatory Commission issued an opinion disagreeing that the RAOI would effectively improve the postal network.[11] A moratorium was placed on closing the post offices on the RAOI list and the USPS ultimately scrapped the RAIO and in 2012 offered a new plan called the POStPlan.

The Post Office Structure Plan (POStPlan) would reduce hours of operation at more than thirteen thousand post offices nationwide, replace postmasters at these post offices with part-time workers, and result in reduction-in-force relocations or terminations for other postal employees at the targeted post offices. The proposed POStPlan also called for town hall meetings to get feedback from residents in communities that would feel the effects of the new plan.

The reduction in operating hours concerned community members in North Dakota, and closure of rural post offices in the state remained a possibility since reduced hours of operation could result in loss of post office employees. *The Forum* of Fargo-Moorhead and other newspapers in the state captured some of the pressures of hours reduction: "Postal Cuts Meant to Help Still Hurt:

[6]United States Postal Service (September 6, 2011), "Postmaster General/CEO Patrick R. Donahoe Before the Committee on Homeland Security and Governmental Affairs," http://about.usps.com/news/speeches/2011/pr11_pmg0906.htm.

[7]United States Postal Service (n.d.), "About," "Retiree Health Benefits Prefunding," http://about.usps.com/who-we-are/financials/annual-reports/fy2010/ar2010_4_002.htm.

[8]United States Postal Service (September 6, 2011), "Postal Service on the Brink of Default," https://about.usps.com/news/national-releases/2011/pr11_102.htm

[9]United States Postal Service (n.d.), "Expanding Access," http://about.usps.com/pcc-insider/2011/pcc_0729.htm.

[10]See Appendix B: Post Offices Named on the 2011 RAOI Closings List. United States Postal Service (n.d.), "Expanded Access Study List. North Dakota," http://about.usps.com/news/electronic-press-kits/expandedaccess/states/northdakota.htm. See also http://savethepostoffice.com/summary-july-2011-closing-lists/

[11]The RAOI Advisory Opinion (December 30, 2011), http://www.savethepostoffice.com/raoi-advisory-opinion-transformative-moment-or-bump-road.

Changes to Strip Many Rural Post Offices of Experienced Hands Behind the Counter" (10/10/2012), "Thompson Plans Rally for its Local Post Office" (10/19/2012), and "Postal Service Seeks to 'restore faith' of Oil Patch Customers" (01/10/2013).

In 2015, the USPS entered phase two of POSt-Plan, reviewing an additional five thousand post offices around the country for reduced hours and staffing. Citizens, postal employees, and congressional delegations from rural areas continued to resist the deconstruction of the postal service that for generations has represented a lifeline for rural communities. In July 2015, senators from North Dakota, Montana, Missouri, and Michigan introduced the Rural Postal Act, designed to increase protections for rural post offices and improve rural mail service.[12] In 2017, the Postal Service Reform Act (H.R. 756) was introduced with the intention of ensuring the long-term solvency of the USPS.

From the seventy-six post offices on the original RAOI closings list, we interviewed thirty-one individuals regarding twenty-three of those post offices. We interviewed an additional nine people about twelve post offices that were not on the closures list.[13] We conducted interviews by calling individuals on a previously obtained list or through an interviewee providing the name of a potential interviewee in another town. As seen in the map on page xix, we made an effort to distribute our interviews geographically across the state. Our interviewees were current or retired postal employees and community members.

Our study was conducted under the auspices of the Institutional Review Boards at the University of North Dakota, Minnesota State University Moorhead, and Minot State University. Financial support for the research phase of the project was provided by Minnesota State University Moorhead and the University of North Dakota.

Wayne Gudmundson took photographs of thirty-seven interviewees and all seventy-six of the post offices on the RAOI closings list. All interviewees except two gave their written consent for the content of their interviews to be used in any presentations or publications resulting from the project. All interviewees except three gave written consent for their photographs to be used. Interviews were audiotaped, transcribed, and analyzed using a grounded theory approach.[14] From this process emerged a list of the roles performed by post offices in rural communities

Going into the project, we had some idea of the importance of rural post offices, but through our conversations with individuals across the state, we came to realize that rural post offices and postal employees are not just vehicles for letter and package delivery—they are also dynamic representatives and reinforcements of the vitality and cohesion of a community. The words of rural North Dakotans in the following chapters prove this assertion, and we were honored to have the opportunity to record them. *The Prairie Post Office* is

[12]Heidi Heitkamp (July 9, 2015), "Heitkamp Introduces New Bill," https://www.heitkamp.senate.gov/public/index.cfm/press-releases?ID=8d9dbdaa-1fe1-4802-82c2-14ff908941ca

[13]In the chapters that follow, most interviewees are referenced by the title they held at the time of the interviews.

[14]K. Charmaz, "Grounded Theory: Objectivist and Constructivist Methods," in *Handbook of Qualitative Research*, 2nd Edition, ed. By N. K Denzin and Y. S. Lincoln (London: Sage Publications, 2000).

North Dakota State Map

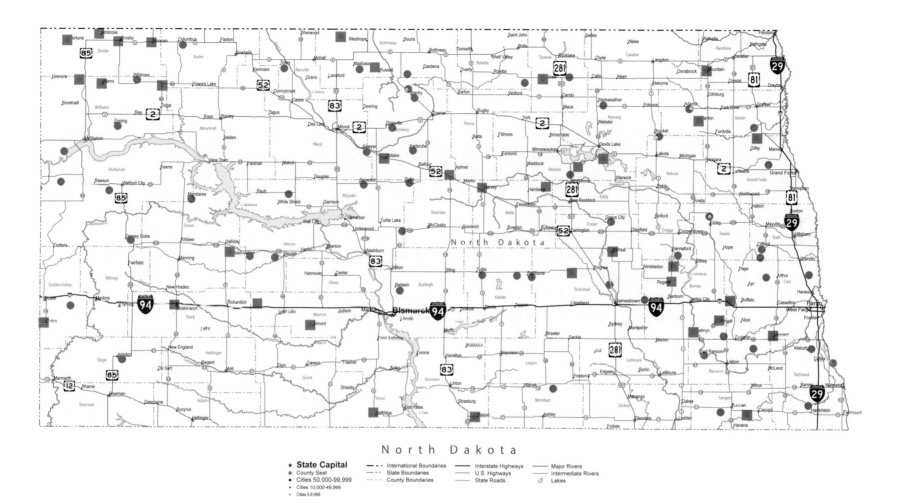

North Dakota

★ **State Capital**
⊚ County Seat
● Cities 50,000-99,999
• Cities 10,000-49,999
· Cities 0-9,999

—·· — International Boundaries
—·—· State Boundaries
—··—·· County Boundaries

——— Interstate Highways
——— U.S. Highways
——— State Roads

——— Major Rivers
——— Intermediate Rivers
⬳ Lakes

● 2011 Closure List; Retail Access Optimization Initiative (RAOI)

▦ Interviews about post offices on Closure List

▦ Interviews about post offices not on Closure List

our tribute to rural post offices and postal employees everywhere, and we intend for it to support the efforts to ensure that rural mail delivery and post offices are not only preserved, but thrive.

In chapter one, Kevin Carvell provides the history of mail delivery in Dakota Territory and the State of North Dakota. Subsequent chapters highlight the roles played by rural post offices and postal employees. These are the roles that emerged most prominently in our interviews with individuals across the state (and are not in order of significance or priority): time-honored public service, information and referral, social, economic, deliverer of basic necessities, and symbolic. We end *The Prairie Post Office* with some final observations about the role of the post office and postal employees in rural North Dakota and elsewhere.

Statement by Wayne Gudmundson

As a photographer, I have traveled North Dakota for more than forty years photographing German-Russian grave markers, two oil booms (numbers two and three), the Garrison Diversion project, an Icelandic community in the northeast corner where my paternal great-grandparents homesteaded, the southeast corner where my maternal great-grandparents homesteaded, and two different book projects that dealt more generally with the cultural landscape of the state. When I was asked to think about the role of post offices in rural North Dakota and to make photographs of the structures and selected individuals in some of those communities, the answer was quite simple. How could I not be interested in this major thread in the social fabric of this region?

Bibliography

Boyd, D. and Chen, K. n.d.. "The History and Experience of African Americans in America's Postal Service," Smithsonian National Postal Museum. http://postalmuseum.si.edu/AfricanAmericanhistory/p11.html

Charmaz, K. 2000. Grounded theory: "Objectivist and constructivist methods." In Denzin N. K. and Y. S. Lincoln (Eds.), *Handbook of qualitative research*, (2nd ed.). London: Sage Publications.

Heidi Heitkamp. July 9, 2015. "Heitkamp Introduces New Bill." https://www.heitkamp.senate.gov/public/index.cfm/press-releases?ID=8d9dbdaa-1fe1-4802-82c2-14ff908941ca

Office of the Inspector General. February 28, 2011. "A Study of the Risks and Consequences of the USPS OIG's Proposals to Change USPS's Funding of Retiree Benefits. Shifting Costs from USPS Ratepayers to Taxpayers." https://www.opm.gov/our-inspector-general/reports/2011/opm_oig_study_of_usps_oig_proposalsfeb282011.pdf

The RAOI Advisory Opinion. December 30, 2011. http://www.savethepostoffice.com/raoi-advisory-opinion-transformative-moment-or-bump-road

United States Code. 2013 Edition. Title 39. § 101. "Postal policy." http://www.gpo.gov/fdsys/pkg/USCODE-2013-title39/html/USCODE-2013-title39.htm

United States Postal Service. n.d.. *The United States Postal Service: An American History. 1775-2006.* Government Relations, United States Postal Service: Washington, DC.

—. n.d. Expanded Access Study List. North Dakota. http://about.usps.com/news/electronic-press-kits/expandedaccess/states/northdakota.htm

—. n.d. "Expanding Access." http://about.usps.com/pcc-insider/2011/pcc_0729.htm

—. n.d. About. "United States Postal Service." https://about.usps.com/publications/pub100/pub100_036.htm

—. September 6, 2011. "Postal Service on the Brink of Default." https://about.usps.com/news/national-releases/2011/pr11_102.htm

—. September 6, 2011. "Postmaster General/CEO Patrick R. Donahoe Before the Committee on Homeland Security and Governmental Affairs." http://about.usps.com/news/speeches/2011/pr11_pmg0906.htm.

—. n.d. About. "Retiree Health Benefits Prefunding." http://about.usps.com/who-we-are/financials/annual-reports/fy2010/ar2010_4_002.htm

CHAPTER 1

A History of the Postal Service in Northern Dakota Territory and the State of North Dakota

by Kevin Carvell

WHEN JOHN HENRY TAYLOR WAS working the Missouri River in Dakota Territory in the last half of the 1800s, trapping up and down its tributaries, he and other lonely and isolated frontiersmen needed a place to exchange messages and get their mail. And so a hollowed-out hole in an oak tree in the Painted Woods along the river became their postal box.

The Painted Woods were, in fact, a bit of a focal point for early communication. They were along the east side of the Missouri, between what would eventually become the North Dakota towns of Wilton and Washburn. That stretch of the Missouri River bottoms had a history of being used as burial grounds of Native peoples, notably the case of star-crossed lovers, a Mandan woman and a Yanktonai Dakota man.[15] In lieu, however, of graves dug into the earth, their bodies were placed in the branches of cottonwood trees. When the sepulcher trees themselves died, their bark would fall off and the tree trunks, bleached by the sun and weather, would turn white. For Native peoples, these creamy trunks proved excellent canvas upon which to scratch, often in color,

messages and pictures. Thus, the region got its name: Painted Woods.

While Native peoples also communicated by a variety of other means — couriers, smoke signals, blankets waved from high points, pictographs, and shiny surfaces manipulated to catch the sun — mail delivery arrived with the Europeans. The earliest stirrings came courtesy of the Hudson's Bay Company and the North West Company, whose trapping empires encompassed the western realm of the British territories. Prior to the treaty settling the War of 1812, the companies' domains also dipped down into what would become North Dakota. Even for years after the war and the treaty establishing the boundary, area citizens were uncertain of just where the division line, the 49th Parallel, ran.

In the Red River Valley, the most important southern trading outpost of the English fur traders was at Pembina. For years, it was a gateway for mail headed to and from the far-flung outposts of the British Empire's fur trade. Mail regularly traveled via canoe along the water route — an international network of lakes and rivers that stretched west from Lake Superior and Lake Michigan along the US–Canadian border to the Red River Country.

[15]Dakota Wind, "Painted Woods: A Tragic Love Story," *The First Scout*, Wednesday March 30, 2011, http://thefirstscout.blogspot.com/2011/03/painted-woods-tragic-love-story.html.

But well used too were routes from the fur trading settlement of Prairie du Chien in southern Wisconsin and, later, as US expansionism pressed west, from Fort Snelling at the confluence of the Minnesota and Mississippi rivers in Minnesota. From there, carriers went west up the Minnesota River and then north down the Red River to Pembina. Depending upon the season, the mail also took what was called the Woods Route, leaving the Mississippi to head northwest through the forests to what would eventually become Grand Forks and then up the Red River.

Most common in that fur trading era were two outgoing mail and two arriving mail pouches a year—one in the spring and one in the fall. More than one thousand letters and packages might arrive at lonely outposts on one of these eagerly awaited deliveries.

Service was, naturally, uncertain. Addressing a correspondent in 1819, the Catholic priest at Pembina, Father Severe Domoulin, said, "The Vicar General and I wrote you by two express canoes sent by Hudson's Bay Company and I will now take advantage of the North-West Company's express, thinking that perhaps it will arrive before the other even though they are ten to twenty days ahead of it."[16]

Three decades later, Fr. Domoulin's Pembina became the site of the first US Post Office in what is now North Dakota. Although the settlement on the US–Canadian border had existed since 1801, the post office did not begin operations until 1850–51. Its postmaster,

North Dakota's first, was Norman Kittson, an entrepreneurial fur trader.

Incessant flooding forced that post office to move out of the Red River Valley and up the Pembina River to the only other European settlement in all of North Dakota, a place called St. Joseph's, which we now know as Walhalla. Trader Charles Grant became the first postmaster there.

Pembina, however, soon got a post office re-established and one of its early postmasters was another famous name in North Dakota history, fur trader Joseph "Jolly Joe" Rolette. Because he so often had to be away on business (he served in the territorial legislature and also as a customs official), his Métis wife, Angelique Jerome, handled the mail during his absence. Because she could not read English, when postal customers came calling, she would simply direct them to the mound of correspondence and the patrons would be personally responsible for digging through it, looking for anything addressed to them.[17]

After those two pioneer trading post communities, the next locales to obtain post offices were military outposts: Fort Abercrombie in 1860, Fort Rice in 1866, Fort Buford in 1867, and Fort Totten in 1868. Then came postal facilities in pioneer villages—Grand Forks in 1870 and, in 1871, Fargo and Wahpeton, and a handful of now forgotten communities: two Traill County places known as Carlton and Goose River, Oswego near present-day Sheldon in Ransom County, and Rose Point in Walsh County.

---

[16]Murray Campbell, "The Postal History of Red River, British North America," *Manitoba Historical Society*, 22 May 2010, http://www.mhs.mb.ca/docs/transactions/3/postalhistory.shtml.

[17]Ibid.

Getting the mail to the military outposts was a dangerous process. Initially, a privately operated mail route established in 1867 linked Fort Abercrombie to Fort Ransom, Fort Totten, Fort Stevenson, and Fort Buford. Lonely stations manned by just two men were set up every fifty miles. Mail deliveries were scheduled three times a week. But the plan collapsed almost immediately when the employees abandoned their perilous posts or were killed.

The army took over the route, generally sending out two-man parties, usually civilians, once a week. The most hazardous stretch was between Fort Totten at Devils Lake and Fort Stevenson on the Missouri River. The commander at Fort Stevenson, General Philippe Regis de Trobriand, complained in 1867: "MacDonald and one of the half-breeds came back from Fort Totten today, bringing the mail. The trip was not without dangers. Dog Den [the area around today's town of Butte] is a bad place to travel across any time. There the terrain is broken by sharp hills and narrow ravines, very favorable to ambuscades."[18]

In the spring of 1868, two mail carriers, Joe Hamlin and Charlie MacDonald, were killed near Strawberry Lake south of present-day Velva.[19] Sitting Bull's Hunkpapa warriors were patrolling their territory against the early manifestations of white colonization. Ten days later, Hamlin and MacDonald's replacements, John Brown and Joe Martin, were captured and stripped naked in the same locale by the same warriors, but both men managed to get away alive.[20]

A month later, still another mail carrier driving a wagon between Fort Totten and Fort Stevenson was attacked near what is now Maddock. Three of the soldiers escorting him were killed.[21] Slain were Sgt. James Devon and Privates Michael Haffin and Louis Martin. After hiding the mail, the survivors retreated to Fort Totten where a relief column was sent out to pick up the dead and salvage the mail.

The route that went south and east from Fort Totten to Fort Abercrombie was safer, but still dangerous, especially because of snow and bitter cold. So that travelers wouldn't get lost, four-foot-high mounds of dirt were heaped upon high points along the trail. If travelers stood atop one mound, they could spot the next off in the distance.

During a blizzard in the winter of 1869, several mail carriers accompanied by three discharged soldiers were caught by the storm between Forts Stevenson and Totten. Three died and the others were found half dead with their limbs frozen.

Many mail carriers were Native Americans, such as La Bombarde, George Koeplin, Blue Thunder, Cool Hand, Bloody Knife, Strikes Two, and Spotted Eagle. They were generally hired by the US Army and often did double duty as scouts.

In his diary, General de Trobriand wrote repeatedly about his concerns for the mail, showing how important that connection to the world was. In March of 1868, he

---

[18] Lucille Kane, ed., Military Life in Dakota (St. Paul, Alvord Memorial Commission, 1951), 138. The term "half-breed" reflects the attitudes and terminology of the day and does not represent the perspectives of the authors.
[19] Ibid., 287.

[20] Ibid., 287–89.
[21] Ibid., 328.

moaned, "How tired I am . . . of this isolation from the rest of the world to which we are bound only by irregular communications at twenty to forty-day intervals and which leaves us with no news of our relatives, with no correspondence with our friends."[22]

Five years later, in Bismarck, the first arrival of mail at the new post office—the home of Linda Slaughter—created a scene. Since there'd been no mail for weeks, Slaughter had gone for a horseback ride. On her return,

> I saw that the house was surrounded by the entire population of Bismarck, men, women and children, all seemingly in a state of great excitement. I never thought of the mail but concluded that the house must be on fire, and galloped up as fast as my horse could come. In the door stood the mail carrier vigorously defending the mail sack against the attacks of several able-bodied citizens who were trying to take it away from him. I was greeted with a ringing cheer as I came up, and half a dozen pairs of long arms were outstretched to lift me from my horse, and I was carried bodily into the house, the whole crowd bursting in after us with a whoop and a hurrah.

> Those who got letters snatched them up with exclamation of delight and some shed tears of joy. Those who got none were correspondingly depressed and a number came back afterward to be assured once more that there really was no letter for them.[23]

In winter, the military used horse-drawn sleighs and dog sleds, and in the spring and summer steamboats carried the mail on both the Red and Missouri rivers. Beginning in 1859, a stagecoach line delivered the mail between Fort Abercrombie and Fort Garry in Canada. Horsemen and dog teams, including famed scout George Northrup, also carried the mail on that route.

It was not always Native warriors who were of concern. The Montana Vigilantes, led by blood-stained Flopping Bill Cantrell, were supposedly hunting rustlers through Dakota Territory and Montana in 1885, but may have lynched more innocent men than guilty. One victim on their murderous crusade was a blameless Métis mail carrier named Gardupie who was tied up, shot, and thrown in a lake near Dogden Butte.[24]

As the state moved out of its frontier era and into its period of European colonization and settlement, postal officials labored to get mail to a mushrooming population. From just a couple thousand white settlers in the 1870s, the state had more than three hundred thousand by 1900 and almost six hundred thousand by 1910. Mail service expanded in a frenetic, rough and tumble, but still surprisingly effective fashion.

Humble sod homes, homestead shanties, and isolated ranches doubled as prairie post offices. At Ranger, in the Badlands, an old sheepherder's wagon served as the post office in the 1920s. And before Grassy Butte got its famous sod post office, bags that carried each owner's brand were filled with mail and hung on a post for settlers to collect. On occasion,

[22]Ibid., 237–38.

[23]Linda W. Slaughter, *Fortress to Farm or Twenty-three Years on the Frontier* (New York: Exposition Press, 1972), 137–38.

[24]Joseph Henry Taylor, *Frontier and Indian Life and Kaleidoscopic Lives* (Valley City: Washburn's Fiftieth Anniversary Committee, 1932), 176.

however, range cattle would disturb the bags and mail blew across the countryside.

At Rhame is Post Office Butte. Before the town began, outgoing mail was lodged under a rock ledge on the butte. When travelers headed north to Medora or Dickinson (fifty to seventy-five miles), they would gather up the accumulated letters for delivery to postal officials.

Since many of the remote post offices did little business, some postmasters could not be troubled to stay at their duty stations all day. When carrier Frank Bryant traveled his route between Napoleon and Ashley, he sometimes found the post office in a ranch house called Youngstown locked up. That did not discourage him—he would wiggle in through a window, make the mail exchange, swipe a can of tomatoes to eat, and be on his way.[25]

In Griggs County, the first postmaster was Frank Taper. He operated the Durham post office from the home of his sister and brother-in-law, the Andrew Durhams, who were hunters and trappers on the Sheyenne River. After an argument during which the brother-in-law brandished a pistol, Taper grabbed the mail and fled to a neighbor's. The next day, his sister and brother-in-law, both now armed, seized the mail back.[26] Postmaster Taper was not heard of again.

So important was mail service that anxious neighbors in the Badlands seventeen miles south of Medora agreed in 1908 that they would personally put an addi-

tion on Luroff and Maggie Holdren's log cabin at Hanly so it could house a post office. It did business until 1920.

Providing a post office out of one's home was more often altruistic than for monetary gain, recalled Harold Kildahl, whose family settled northwest of Devils Lake in 1883:

> The post office proved to be a nuisance, more trouble and bother than it was worth. While we were proud to be on the map, even a very small map, when the post office was moved to Maza, it proved to be a relief. Somebody had to be on hand constantly to serve the occasional patron, but there was little if anything in it financially. To convey some idea of the small volume of post office business transacted, I received a fancy check from Washington in the amount of 18 cents for three months work.[27]

To cobble together a living, a postmaster had to do more than just handle the mail. In Fargo's first days, a sign over the door of Postmaster Gordon Keeney's tiny building (120 square feet) declared it to be the postal service while a marker on the door said it was the land office and a window banner indicated it was also the home of his law practice. In addition, it was Keeney's dwelling place and that of a friend, and on the roof, he grew lettuce. But before he had the building, he was a walking post office, carrying the mail around in his coat pockets until he met his postal patrons.[28]

Many early post offices were located inside a business, usually a general store, but sometimes a

[25] Nina Farley Wishek, *Along the Trails of Yesterday* (Ashley, ND: *The Ashley Tribune*, 1941), 63.

[26] *Griggs County History* (Dallas, TX: Griggs County Heritage Book Committee, 1976), 6.

[27] Harold B. Kildahl, Sr., "Westward We Came," *North Dakota History* (Winter 1994): 17.

[28] Clarence A. Glasrud, ed., *Roy Johnson's Red River Valley* (Moorhead, MN: Red River Valley Historical Society, 1982), 331

hotel or other establishment. And although the mail business wasn't particularly lucrative, the store owner had a steady stream of postal customers coming through his doors who might also buy something from his retail stock.

Known as Litchville, Jacob Hanson's combined store and post office was in LaMoure County. But when in 1900 he learned that the railroad was laying track six miles north in Barnes County, he hoisted up his building in the middle of the night and moved it.[29] He kept the name Litchville, but forgot for a year to tell postal officials that he had transplanted their facility into another county.

Railroads were the natural way to get the mail transferred from point to point. But trains didn't stop regularly at the smallest prairie places. To get the mail aboard, the mailbag from the post office was hung on a pole that extended next to the tracks and was snatched as the train roared through.

But Si Jordan, the depot agent at Oriska, was napping when the Northern Pacific came through one day. And he was without his pants, having taken them off to prevent them from wrinkling while he slept. Hearing the train whistle, Jordan awoke with a start, grabbed his pants in one hand and the mailbag in the other, and sprinted out to the platform to see the train rumbling by. And, just in time, he tightly held onto the mail bag and threw his pants on board. (Two days later, when the train made its return trip, his pants were thrown off.)[30]

There were other hazards. Post offices suffered late night burglaries and daytime stickups. And, sometimes, fleas. At Williston, coyote pelts were being shipped out when one parcel broke open and thousands of fleas escaped.[31] To rid himself of the curse, postal employee Orville Springer had to take numerous baths in kerosene.

All told, North Dakota had almost two thousand post offices at one time or another. The peak year was 1900 when there were eight hundred seventy. As settlers from the final burst of homesteading almost immediately began to thin out and farms consolidated, prairie post offices started their decline.

Several other factors played critical roles. The advent of rural free delivery to the front yard of most farms and ranches diminished the necessity of a nearby post office. Those rural carriers picked up outgoing letters and packages and even sold postage for them. And the widespread use of automobiles dramatically extended the range of rural carriers and also the ability of prairie postal patrons to access a distant post office.

With the improvement of automobiles and, equally important, roads and highways, the rural population was no longer tied to the nearest village and its abbreviated retail services. Those wide spots in the road declined and their stores shuttered. Often, the last establishments left standing were the post office and a tavern. Patrons always fought the closing of their handy local post office, but they were almost inevitably unsuccessful.

In recent years, the postal service has been under enormous economic pressure to close even more post offices. Part of that comes from the tectonic shift in

[29]*Litchville, North Dakota, 1900–2000* (Jamestown, ND: Litchville History Book Committee, 2000), 295–96.

[30]John A. Conway, ed., *Oriska 1881–1981* (Fargo, ND: Oriska History Committee, 1980), 137.

[31]William E. Shemorry, *Best of the Best Little Stories of the Twentieth Century* (Williston, ND: Shemorry Photo and Publications, 1999), 130–31.

package and correspondence delivery. Alternatives like FedEx and UPS, cheap long distance telephone rates, and the explosion of the internet slice into the post office's traditional business.

Part of the dilemma comes from the government itself. In 1971, following the Postal Reorganization Act of 1970, when the Post Office became the quasi-independent US Postal Service, it was cut off from government support. Public service seemed no longer top priority. Instead, the paramount consideration was the need to maximize income. That led to increases in rates, declines in service, and a further shuttering of post offices. More recently, a conservative Congress hostile to public postal service operations created another enormous economic burden by ordering the agency to prepay all its pension obligations for fifty to seventy-five years into the future, a demand made on no other public entity or private corporation.[32]

Nonetheless, North Dakota still had four hundred fifty towns with post offices in 1985 and today, over thirty years later, almost three hundred. A recent attempt to padlock seventy-six of those was beaten back by an outcry from those communities, but the Postal Service, using a back-door approach, cut the business hours of many. Some locations were left operating as little as two hours a day.

Post offices have been an essential component of a vibrant community life, a critical player in stitching together the nation. Particularly in the wide spots along the prairie roads, the hamlets and small towns, the post office has been the heart and the core of the community. No other governmental function has so proven itself such a vital element in the construction and maintenance of democracy, serving every citizen equally, touching the life of every American.

---

[32]"Waiting for Deliverance," *The Economist*, http://www.economist.com/node/21554221.

Selected Bibliography

Aaberg, Gwendolyn M. *The RFD Golden Jubilee 1896–1946*, n.p., 1946.

Campbell, Murray, MD. "The Postal History of Red River, British North America," Manitoba Historical Society, 2 May 2010.

Conway, John A., ed. *Oriska 1881–1981*. Fargo, ND: Oriska History Committee, 1980.

De Noyer, Charles. "The History of Fort Totten." *Collections of the State Historical Society of North Dakota, Vol. III*. ed. O.G. Libby. Bismarck, ND [State Historical Society], 1910.

Farley, James A. "Advertisement Inviting Proposals for Carrying the Mails of the United States on Star Routes in the State of North Dakota from July 1, 1934, to June 30, 1938." Washington: US Government Printing Office, 1933.

Fiftieth Anniversary Rhame, North Dakota 1908–1958. n.p.: Friendly City Club, 1958.

Fuglie, Jim. "Who Owns Your Post Office." *The Prairie Blog*. 6 Dec. 2011. http://theprairieblog.areavoices.com/2011/12/06/who-owns-your-post-office/

Glasrud, Clarence, ed. *Roy Johnson's Red River Valley*. Moorhead, MN: Red River Valley Historical Society, 1982.

Goplin, Arnold O. "The Historical Significance of Fort Lincoln State Park." *North Dakota History*. Oct. 1946: 151–221.

Grassy Butte News 1916-1922. n.p.: Grassy Butte History Committee, n.d.

Griggs County Heritage. Dallas: Griggs County Heritage Book Committee, 1976.

Johnson, Eleanor, Agnes Palanuk, and Esther Swenson, eds. *Echoing Trails*. Fargo, ND: Billings County Historical Society, 1979.

Kane, Lucille M., ed. *Military Life in Dakota*. St. Paul: Alvord Memorial Commission, 1951.

Kildahl, Harold B., Sr. "Westward We Came." *North Dakota History*. Winter 1994: 9-21.

Larson, Arthur J. "The Northwestern Express and Transportation Company." *North Dakota Historical Quarterly*. Oct. 1931–July 1932: 42-62.

Litchville, North Dakota 1900–2000. Jamestown, ND: Litchville History Book Committee, 2000.

Margolis, Richard J. *At the Crossroads, An Inquiry Into Rural Post Offices and the Communities They Serve*. Washington: US Postal Rate Commission, 1982.

Mattison, Ray. "Fort Rice — North Dakota's First Missouri River Military Post." North Dakota History. Apr. 1953: 87–108.

Mattison, Ray. "Old Fort Stevenson." *North Dakota History*. Apr.–July 1951: 53–91.

Patera, Alan H. and John S. Gallagher. *North Dakota Post Offices 1850–1982*. Burtonsville, MD: The Depot, 1982.

Pfaller, Louis, Reverend. "The Fort Keogh to Bismarck Stage Route." *North Dakota History*. July 1954: 91–125

Plath, Agnes. *North Dakota Centennial on Philately*. n.p.: Self-published, 1989.

Reid, Russell. "Diary of Ferdinand A. Van Ostrand." *North Dakota Historical Quarterly*. Jan. 1943: 3–46.

Rein, Lisa. "Postal Service Names 3,700 Post Offices that Could be Closed." Washington Post.com. 26 July 2011. https://www.washingtonpost.com/politics/postal-service-names-3700-post-offices-that-could-be-closed/2011/07/26/gIQARk3tbl_story.html?utm_term=.cc42d2f36b30

Shemorry, William E. *Best of the Best Little Stories of the Twentieth Century*. Williston, ND: Shemorry Photo and Publications, 1999.

Slaughter, Linda W. "Fort Abercrombie." *Collections of the State Historical Society of North Dakota Vol. I*. ed. O.G. Libby. Bismarck, ND: [State Historical Society], 1910.

Slaughter, Linda W. *Fortress to Farm or Twenty-three Years on the Frontier*. New York: Exposition Press, 1972.

Slope Saga, Bowman, ND: Slope Saga Committee, 1976.

Taylor, Joseph Henry. *Frontier and Indian Life and Kaleidoscopic Lives*. 1895 and 1902. Reprint. Valley City, ND: Washburn's 50th Anniversary Committee, 1932.

Tunwéya Thokáheya, *The First Scout* website. http://thefirstscout.blogspot.com/

Upgren, Ted. "Neither Rain, Nor Heat, Nor Gloom of Night." *North Dakota Horizons*. Fall 1976: 26-31.

Utley, Robert. *The Lance and the Shield*. New York: Henry Holt, 1993, "Waiting for Deliverance." *The Economist*. 5 May 2012.

Wick, Douglas A. *North Dakota Place Names*. Bismarck, ND: Hedmarken Collectibles, 1988.

Winship, George B. "Forty Years of Development of the Red River Valley." *History of the Red River Valley*. Grand Forks, ND, and Chicago: Herald Printing and C.F. Cooper, 1900.

Wishek, Nina Farley. *Along the Trails of Yesterday*. Ashley, ND: Ashley Tribune, 1941.

Wright, Dana. "The Fort Totten-Fort Stevenson Trail 1867–1872." *North Dakota History*. Apr. 1952: 67–86.

Wright, Dana. "Military Trails in Dakota — The Fort Totten-Abercrombie Trail." *North Dakota History*. Jan.–Apr. 1946: 80–95.

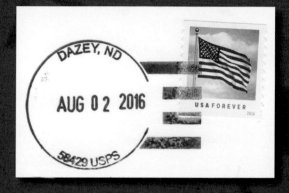

CHAPTER 2

The Role of the Prairie Post Office in Providing Time-Honored Public Service

"I think it's important to keep these services open to the people . . .
to accommodate the people of the community."

— Philip Quick, Rural Letter Carrier, Dazey

THE VIEW OF THE POST office as providing a public service was reinforced repeatedly in our interview conversations. Interviewees made a point of saying that "it's the United States Postal *Service*," emphasizing the fact that they were part of a communication system that guaranteed a reliable and convenient social benefit to virtually every household in the nation. They made note of the fact that this service is unique in the United States Postal Service — even the private delivery companies (such as UPS and FedEx) left packages at the local post office to ensure "last mile delivery" by USPS letter carriers to rural route addresses. Interviewees also emphasized that mail service included a focus on safety and security — the all-encompassing notion of the "sanctity of the mail" — via the USPS's own mail safety programs and the Postal Inspection Service (one of the oldest federal law enforcement agencies in the country).

The United States Postal Service has seen a decrease in its First Class mail volume (e.g., letters, bills, postcards) as a result of ever-expanding digital forms of communication, such as e-mail and social media. Several interviewees, however, made a point of highlighting the historic and continuing function of the rural post office as a vehicle for print communication between people who may be separated by hundreds of miles or just a few blocks.

In addition to highlighting the safe and reliable communication network provided by the national postal service, interviewees also emphasized their individual roles in serving both this network and the communities in which they lived and worked. First and foremost, postal employees detailed the numerous and varied responsibilities associated with working in the post office and on rural mail routes. These responsibilities included selling postage and other products, sorting and scanning incoming and outgoing mail, maintaining financial records, ordering supplies, delivering mail, responding to correspondence from district offices, and even housekeeping and some building and grounds maintenance. If an employee worked for any length of time at the post office, she often had to learn, on very short notice, new computer programs and scanning systems related to keeping records and tracking the mail. Postmasters from neighboring towns would often assist each other with learning these systems and would rely on each other for support with other aspects of the work. In other words, a community not only benefitted from the service provided by its postmaster, but a rural network of postal employees was available to ensure that service to any one community was not interrupted.

The articulation of work as *service*, however, was not simply related to their employment in a government department with the word "service" in its title. The prominence of service was more clearly connected to the postal employees' status as community members. Their customers were people they had known since child-hood, attended church with, or learned from in school. The bond they felt with their communities, and the trust placed in them by community residents, reinforced their sense of commitment to the work as service. They took pride in their work as postal employees, but were also proud of how their work contributed to and supported the lives of the people in their communities.

Rutland Community Members: Back—Cal Jacobson, Bill Anderson, Paul Anderson; Front—Beverly Kulzer, Ione Pherson (Rutland Postmaster), Lois Nelson, Betty Nelson

"I think it is the universality of the post office—that the postal service reaches from Rutland, North Dakota, to Washington, DC, to Los Angeles, California, and from there, here. It's all over, every community in the country is served by it."

—Bill Anderson, Community Member, Rutland

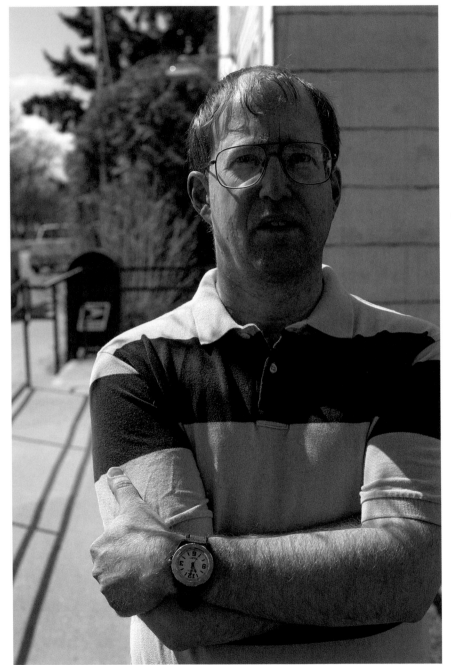

"Benjamin Franklin started this and he figured if you are going to have a country and have uniform commerce throughout the country, you have to have this."

— Scott Heck, Former Officer-in-Charge, Mountain

Scott Heck, Former Officer-in-Charge, Mountain

Brad Mincher, Community Member, Anamoose

"If you look at every other business that went private, some of them work and some of them don't. Some of them are shoddy in their operations. But the post office, at least to me, is always consistent."

— Brad Mincher, Community Member, Anamoose

Post Office, Terrell Avenue, Golva

"I think people just take for granted that they pay for their postage and you take the package and it gets there."

— Pam Beach, Postmaster Relief, Golva

"[The private carriers] would never give the service that we do, and we have the protection of our law enforcement postal inspectors; they take care of the mail and anything that's going wrong."

— Irene Colby, Retired Postmaster, Voltaire

Irene Colby, Retired Postmaster, Voltaire (At the time of her retirement, Mrs. Colby was the longest serving postmaster in North Dakota, having been appointed by President John F. Kennedy in 1962.)

Post Office, Central Avenue, Dodge

"What I like about small towns is people send cards to each other all the time. In town, there is the Sunshine Club and they get quite a few little cards, and handmade cards too. There's a stamp club and they are very, very social. The Sunshine Club will send thank you cards for people coming over and helping them calve and do all the farm stuff."

— Becky Pugliese, Postmaster Relief, Dodge

"We had such a support field out there, if you didn't want to always bother the individuals in the district office you'd call your friends: 'Did you figure this out?' 'Do you know how to do this?' And if you knew, you let them know. You were always there as a backup for everybody."

—Lenora Mosset, Retired Postmaster, Selfridge

Lenora Mosset, Retired Postmaster, Selfridge

Mark Kostelecky, Rural Letter Carrier, Dickinson

"I hope I represent service and I hope that I represent a friendly face—you know, somebody they can count on and know that I'll be there to provide them service."

—Mark Kostelecky, Rural Letter Carrier, Dickinson

Wanda Wehrman, Retired Postmaster, Fortuna

"I don't think there was ever a day that I dreaded getting up and going to work. [During a blizzard,] I would get in my car and I would turn around and come back. My husband took me many times."

— Wanda Wehrman, Retired Postmaster, Fortuna

Shannon Gessner, Postmaster, Newburg

"[It's] that satisfaction I get when I deliver the wedding announcements that came from the printer, the letter for grandpa that came and it has a colored drawing in it. The baby chicks that come for the home-schooled kids. I deliver so much more than bills and I do so much more than sell stamps. My job is so fulfilling. I love my job so much."

— Shannon Gessner, Postmaster, Newburg

Postal employees we interviewed emphasized their love of the work they did or continue to do. The work was not always easy since it called for frequent knowledge and skill upgrades, expectations of getting to and staying at work in all kinds of weather, and the frequent pressures of tracking and reporting deadlines. It was clear that postal interviewees took very seriously the purpose of the Postal Service to "provide prompt, reliable, and efficient services to patrons." But they also took seriously the fact that the services they provided helped meet the varied needs of local businesses, churches, schools, families, and individual residents. They were gratified to play a role in meeting these needs and proud to be part of a long-standing and time-honored public service.

CHAPTER 3

The Information and Referral Role
of the Prairie Post Office

"A lot of people come in and ask directions on how to get to certain places
and I [tell them]. I've had people come in and ask where the cemetery is
and they want to know if so-and-so is buried out there."

—Sharon Tennyson, Officer-in-Charge, Antler

MAIL DELIVERY IS A PRIMARY element of the United States Postal Service in urban, suburban, and rural areas across the country. The post office also serves for many people as a source for tax forms, contact information of elected officials, and other government information. In rural areas, these and other functions are especially important to community vitality because few alternatives exist. Indeed, our interviews revealed that the post office or the rural letter carrier was often the only government institution with which residents would have regular contact. Moreover, the post office was viewed as a trusted source for local information such as directions, where former residents might be buried, resources for new community members, and reports of births, deaths, or illnesses of current or recent residents.

This information and referral role of the prairie post office captures an interesting blend of the bureaucratic focus of official USPS mission and operating procedures and the neighborliness of how the local post office fulfilled that mission. While nearly all of the postal employees with whom we spoke talked of the pride they took in working with the USPS, that pride seemed to be as, or more, rooted in their connections to the community and the information and resources they could provide because of those connections.

Joanne Moreland, Retired Postmaster, Inkster

"I had a lot of people that would come in and ask for some of the old pioneer names. Since I lived here all my life and my dad knew everybody around here, I heard a lot of talk about these different people, and I could tell them whether they were buried in the Inkster cemetery."

—Joanne Moreland, Retired Postmaster, Inkster

Post Office, Main Street, Voltaire

"In the early days of the United Parcel Service [UPS], they always stopped at the post office for directions. Some were not happy about that but I always helped them out. They were also customers of the postal service. They have a contract with the postal service at this time where they leave some parcels with [the rural letter carrier] to deliver because it's more convenient I guess. [T]he postal service goes everywhere you know — every residence in the nation every day. No one else can say that."

— Irene Colby, Retired Postmaster, Voltaire

"The thing is, we don't have a paper, we don't have a radio station. They will come in and look [at the community bulletin board] and they'll see what's going on that they otherwise wouldn't know about."

—Kathy Aarseth, Postmaster, Fingal

Kathy Aarseth, Postmaster, Fingal

"[The post office] is the only place to stop, the only open door on Main Street."

— Sharon Coleman, Postmaster, Kathryn

Sharon Coleman, Postmaster, Kathryn

Post Office, Main Avenue, Mountain

"[The post office is a kind of] welcome wagon—somebody would move into the community and they would ask, 'who do I talk to about getting power activated on the house?' They are looking for apartments, a house to rent, or maybe a house to buy. And I give them a few tips like, 'there are places you don't want to live because it's in the flood plain.' People would come in and ask 'what cell phone service works here?'"

—Scott Heck, Former Officer-in-Charge, Mountain

Post Office, Central Avenue, Dodge

"The first thing you do when you move to a town is you get a post office box or you change your address. The mail carrier is one of the first people you meet."

— Becky Pugliese, Officer-in-Charge, Dodge

"We're a source of information for all different kinds of things. Some people you help find phone numbers; sometimes you help figure out [which] department of government you should go to for whatever it is they're looking for."

—Nancy Covell, Postmaster, Leonard

Nancy Covell, Postmaster, Leonard

Florence Oakland, Retired Postmaster, Bisbee

"[T]he postmaster in these small towns not only represents the federal government but they are the go-to person if people have questions. It's amazing the number of problems and questions people come into the post office with because there is nobody else to ask these questions to."

—Florence Oakland, Retired Postmaster, Bisbee

Phyllis Quick, Retired Postmaster, Rogers

"[A role of the post office] is to accommodate the people of the community. If they had trouble, they think, 'I will call so and so [at the PO] to find out about rules or regulations or public law.'"

—Phyllis Quick, Retired Postmaster, Rogers

Even in a small community, keeping up with civic news and personal news of one's neighbors can be a challenge. The rural post office emerges as an important intersection in the formal and informal networks at a time when other rural points of connection, such as the local cafe and school, are disappearing. Since many of the postal employees we interviewed were long-time residents, local knowledge and history is literally embodied in the post office.

CHAPTER 4

The Social Role of the Prairie Post Office

"It's their center of town, their meeting place. It's where you see people, and if Ida didn't come up this morning at 9:12, hey, somebody better check on her—she must be sick. And that's what they do."

— Art Prom, Retired Postmaster, Harvey

THE SOCIAL ROLE OF THE prairie post office cannot be overstated. Particularly in rural settings, the post office serves as a social gathering place and as a venue for social support. "The hub of the community" and "lifeline" were frequent terms used to reference the rural post office.

As a gathering place, the post office is a location for people to meet, catch up on personal news, learn of events taking place, and reinforce community bonds. This function is particularly important when other gathering places such as churches, schools, and community centers have been closed. In some cases, people begin gathering at the post office every day before the mail is available and chat with each other while the postmaster distributes the mail to individual boxes. After the mail is picked up, a group of people may move to the local cafe for further conversation. In addition, the post office is a place where family members from a farm or ranch who come to mail a package may encounter someone they have not seen in a while.

The role of the rural post office as a gathering place is often enhanced by the personality and activities of the postmaster, frequently a woman, who engages in acts of hospitality designed to create a welcoming or festive atmosphere. Several of the interviewees mentioned buying treats or items with their own money in order to enliven the spirit of a holiday.

The rural post office and its employees also provide a type of social support service—a role that reflects the mutual aid aspect of rural relationships. Postal employees we interviewed often performed "good neighbor" tasks, such as locating someone if an item was forgotten at the post office, assisting older residents with getting packages to and from their cars, and even providing pet care or finding homes for stray animals. In addition, postal employees functioned in more substantive ways as social supports, going beyond their job descriptions to help and find help for the residents of their communities. Postal employees were particularly concerned about the older residents in their communities, and they described the post office as serving an important role in helping older persons stay physically active and socially involved.

"[The post office] is the medical center, it's the social center, and it's the place they get their mail."

— Art Prom, Retired Postmaster, Harvey

Art Prom, Retired Postmaster, Harvey

"It's a place where people meet and everybody comes together at the post office. On Valentine's Day every year, I would have a drawing for a big chocolate heart at the post office. And then I would have all the kids in the community make valentines and I would decorate the post office with valentines. And that's the same way with Christmas — I would buy postal products and would give away stamps; I would give away a lot of postal products. It would probably run me about $100.00."

— Linda Ehrhardt, Retired Postmaster, Almont

Linda Ehrhardt, Retired Postmaster, Almont

Post Office, 3rd Street, Fingal

"Well, they meet and they visit. I don't think they plan to be here but when they come, sometimes it's the only time they get to see each other."

—Kathy Aarseth, Postmaster, Fingal

"That bench out there, that's not there for people to lay their mail on. People sit on that bench and they visit."

— Shannon Gessner, Postmaster, Newburgh

Donna Mae O'Connor, Retired Operator of Community Post Office, Bremen

"The mail would come in at a certain time and people would sit and wait until the mail came, so they would communicate. They would go early because that way they knew they would get a chance to see somebody."

—Donna Mae O'Connor, Retired operator of a Community Post Office, which was located in her home in Bremen

"For a lot of [postal customers] in this area, the post office is their only contact with a person, especially seniors if they are living alone or something, so you are kind of doing a good deed talking to them. And we've had so many oil workers who are from South Carolina or wherever; they just gobble it up because you remember them by first name, you smile, you talk to them every day. And that means a lot because they are away from home and their families."

—Judy Legaard, Retired Postmaster, Fortuna

Judy Legaard, Retired Postmaster, Fortuna

Joanne Moreland (at left), Retired Postmaster, Inkster, with friend and former Inkster postal employee Melva Becker

"It was a hub of the community after the store closed. I made coffee for years, at my own expense. There was one fellow—I don't think he ever made coffee at home. He came up and had his cup of coffee in the morning at the post office and that was it for the day. Oh and holidays, or if there was somebody's birthday or something, I'd bake a cake and bring it in and have cake and coffee."

—Joanne Moreland, Retired Postmaster, Inkster

"The son that came in for his mother, he was on vacation and needed somebody to watch his cat so he asked me to do it. I left the post office at the end of the day, then I'd go to his house and take care of his cat for him."

— Valerie Weidrich, Officer-in-Charge, Kensal

Valerie Weidrich, Officer-in-Charge, Kensal

Gail Beneda, Postmaster, Lankin

"In December I would always have a customer appreciation day and I'd bring bars and cookies and coffee and cider or something, or put out some candy at Valentine's Day and Halloween. And that's all at your own expense."

— Gail Beneda, Postmaster, Lankin

Valerie Treesoul, Postmaster Relief, Woodworth

"It's knowing about the community, knowing when someone's out of town, why their mail is backed up. Knowing family, who to contact if there's something going on."

—Valerie Treesoul, Postmaster Relief, Woodworth

Mailbox, Mountain Post Office

"Some of the elderly people that live on their own, many of them never kept track of their medications so sometimes they would come in and say 'my medication didn't come in.' So out of concern we would contact one of their relatives and say, 'Your mother is out of her diabetic medication,' or 'Your dad is in here, and he's out of blood thinners or something. Did you know this?'"

— Scott Heck, Former Officer-in-Charge, Mountain

Donna Walker and Karen Keller, Community Members, Hague

The Prairie Post Office: Enlarging the Common Life in Rural North Dakota

"It's very, very important to them to have [the post office]. It's convenient—they don't have family that comes around and takes care of them. They may not even get a piece of mail, but they are going to the post office, they are going to come to the store, and then they are going to go to the cafe. And that's the highlight of their day. It keeps them thriving. That's the social part."

—Donna Walker, Community Member, Hague

"The older folks have their ways about them. They get their coffee, they go to the post office, they go and visit with people and they walk through and look at people's gardens and they go and have their meal at the town hall and gossip a little, open their mail, take their medicine and go home. It's their routine and the post office is as important to them as going down and playing cards at the general store."

—Becky Pugliese, Postmaster Relief, Dodge

"I have comforted people at my counter that didn't get a Mother's Day card on the Saturday before Mother's Day. And then I took it upon myself to call their kids and say, 'I'm sure you forgot, but . . .' I have celebrated with people that have sent in their last car payment. I have helped package up cookies to send to Desert Storm. . . . This guy across the street—his family had the grocery store across the street. I got my first job from them. He was in the hospital having some knee surgery and I kept track of his mail. He ended up going to the nursing home after that. When he finally came home, I painted on the window, "Welcome Home Mr. T." When he sat in his chair, it's the first thing he saw when he looked out the window, and he cried. And I'd take his mail to him just across the street because that's what the people in Newburg do."

—Shannon Gessner, Postmaster, Newburg

It was evident from our interviews that rural post offices, and the people working in them, function as a kind of social service agency. The post office is a social hub for catching up on local news, determining the well-being of neighbors in and out of town, and enjoying holiday treats provided by postmasters. Walking to the post office to pick up mail helps ensure routine physical activity and social interaction for older residents. In addition, postal employees often function as part of a support system by contacting family members when a resident was in need, offering conversation and attention to someone who was lonely, and providing neighborly services above-and-beyond their job description.

After mail delivery, the social role may be one of the most important roles of the post office, especially in the absence of other gathering places and social support institutions such as churches, voluntary associations, and community centers. In its social role, the rural post office contributes to the mutual support function of the community and serves to help bind the community together.

CHAPTER 5

The Economic Role of the Prairie Post Office

"We have people coming in to mail a package and they might buy something at the grocery store, they might eat lunch at the bar. I'm sure it helps the entire economy of the town even though there are only a couple of businesses here."

—Pam Beach, Postmaster Relief, Golva

CITY PLANNERS AND COMMUNITY development advocates realize that business begets business. Without a critical mass of economic activity, a community's economic vitality is eroded. Moreover, businesses, churches, schools, and municipal agencies all depend on other businesses for office supplies, cleaning products, computers and other equipment, and repair services, among other needs. These dual roles — the catalyst function of a critical mass of going concerns and the support-services function — are especially important in rural areas because of the smaller scale of the local economy. The web of interdependence is more fragile.

Most of the communities in which we interviewed had few businesses or other entities, such as churches or schools, in operation. Some communities face the prospect of their post office closing or having hours of operation reduced; the postal service bureaucracy has assured residents that mail service will not be undermined as a result of these changes, but community members expressed their concern that having a post office nearby was very important. For many, the loss of their local post office would mean a drive of twenty or more miles for the services one can get only at a post office. This would be a particular hardship in winter or during spring floods or for those without access to a car. A reduction in hours also poses a problem in that it is unclear which portion of the day the post office should remain open to meet the needs of the community residents and mail patrons.

The people we interviewed, especially business owners, were particularly concerned about the potential loss of support services. They realize that a loss of the local post office undermines the speed at which parts are delivered from the out-of-town supply shop to the local plumber, the access to the secured-mail services relied on by the local attorney, and the convenient shipping services for the mail-order businesses.

Paul Anderson, Community Member, Rutland

"The window opens at 8:30 and normally people get their mail in the next hour or so. It's a generator of business for the cafe here. It's right next door to the cafe—people get their mail and they'll either have a cup of coffee beforehand or a cup of coffee afterwards."

—Paul Anderson, Community Member, Rutland

"A lot of people are employed at Sun Manufacturing and at Mouse River Outfitters. They need their mail in the morning but they need their mail to go out in the evening too. And not all their mail is always postaged correctly. I have to weigh their packages and tell them how much. They can't be running up here several times a day. And sometimes their mail can't wait until the next day to go out; that's why I'm concerned. What four hours are they going to keep Newburg open—8:00 to 12:00? That's not going to work. The school has mail that needs to go out, Cenex has mail that needs to go out. Noon to 4:00? That's not going to work."

—Shannon Gessner, Postmaster, Newburg

Post Office, 1st Street North, Rutland

"Certainly you can use [UPS or FedEx to] get parts here, but you won't get them until almost a working day later [than the post office]."

—Cal Jacobson, Community Member, Rutland

"The post office offers us a full-time job . . . but there's also two other people that do part-time work in the post office. This gives them an income and puts another little bit of income into the community."

—Paul Anderson, Community Member, Rutland

"I'm an attorney and I need to send documents from place to place, to courts. I need to have verification that those documents have gotten to where they need to go properly and in a timely manner. And the postal service does that and it's right here."

—Bill Anderson, Community Member, Rutland

"There are actually three independent beauty consultants and a couple of other businesses in town. I guess for me it's pretty important that it's here. . . . It's nice and convenient when you have kids that want to take naps so you can just run down, do what you need to do and then run back."

— Melissa Sutton, Community Member, Alamo

Melissa Sutton, Community Member, Alamo

The catalyst function and the business support function of the post office in a local economy are especially vital in small communities. The local business people we interviewed were adamant that access to a post office offers unique advantages. For the plumber relying on delivery of parts from a supply house, the post office can save a whole business day in delivery times relative to private outfits like UPS or FedEx. For an attorney or others relying on registered or certified mail, the post office is the only option. The private carriers do not have the same legal assurance of sanctity and security of the US mail. The lesson here: UPS and FedEx are not perfect, or even adequate, substitutes for the United States Postal Service.

CHAPTER 6

The Role of the Prairie Post Office as a Deliverer of Basic Necessities

"Out here, we don't have a Walmart down the street, we don't have a drugstore down the street, most of the implement dealers with parts for farmers, they're not down the street anymore. The mail is the only way we get those. We need the mail."

—Florence Oakland, Retired Postmaster, Bisbee

THE RURAL POST OFFICE SERVES many of the same functions as a suburban or urban post office; as explained previously, it facilitates the delivery of mail, contributes to an unparalleled distribution network, offers secured-mail services like registered mail, and provides tax forms and other government-related documents and information. Anyone unfamiliar with the Great Plains states may not appreciate that rural communities in a state like North Dakota can be some distance, fifty to one hundred miles, from amenities like a pharmacy, a hardware store, or a large grocery store. Consequently, unlike in suburban areas, the post office and mail delivery are essential means through which rural residents have ready access to needed goods and services.

Because of the relative remoteness of the community or the lack of access to transportation, many people we interviewed in rural communities spoke of mail delivery as a "lifeline." Newspapers, parts for farm equipment, and even baby chicks are delivered through the mail. Increasingly common for people everywhere, medicine and medical supplies are also delivered via the mail. For people in rural areas, however, no alternate source exists other than the mail, and some medications require special handling to avoid extreme heat or cold.

Bridget Johnson, Postmaster, Crosby

"The chickens are mailed and the pheasants and ducks or whatever. We get them in the mail in the spring and then we look in there to see if they are all alive, we shake the box a little bit, and then I usually call the customer and say 'well, out of twenty-five, twenty-three are still kickin'.'"

—Bridget Johnson, Postmaster, Crosby

"The farmers, they need their parts, my people need their medication. We have to drive to get groceries. A lot of people now with insurances running the way they are. . . . they don't give you a week in advance [for a refill]. They will maybe give you two days or three days. [Residents here] need to have their mail and they can't afford to make a trip to Minot to get it. I have seniors in Antler, they car pool to go get groceries. And they can't wait a week to drive to Westhope or to Minot to get their mail. . . . We still have the school here; they need their mail every day. I've come at quarter to eight in the morning and have had farmers standing here waiting because there is that piece that they need so they can get to the field."

— Shannon Gessner, Postmaster, Newburg

Rural Letter Carrier, near Tower City

"I really believe that we are the lifelines for our rural customers. We bring them their medicine, we bring their parcels, their mail, and we also provide a service as far as picking up packages that they want sent out or mail that they need sent out."

— Mark Kostelecky, Rural Letter Carrier, Dickinson

"Once you've lived here and you see what goes on every day, it's hard to explain how important it is to the people. [Outsiders] will say, 'well they don't need to go up there and get their mail.' They don't understand that [the post office] is like a lifeline."

— Donna Walker, Community Member, Hague

"Most people depend on the postal service for their medicine; they depend on the postal service for their parts or whatever else they have coming. A lot of people depend on the post office whether you are a farmer or a retired person living in the community. Everybody depends on that post office to get their mail. Like I say, it's their lifeline."

— Sharon Tennyson, Officer-in-Charge, Antler

Sharon Tennyson, Officer-in-Charge, Antler

Helen Shaw, Community Member, Hague

"I'm a diabetic and I have to have my insulin mailed to me because I can't manage to get over [to the pharmacy in Linton] during the wintertime. Since it's inside [the post office] and it's warm I don't have to worry about my insulin getting frozen.... If I had a mailbox at my house, it would still be unhandy for me because I would still have to get on the [motorized chair] and go out and try to get into my mailbox and no telling how long it would be before I could get out to it.... And [cluster boxes] wouldn't work for me either because when the snow comes, they will have a lot of snow piled up against them and there is no way I can get close enough to get my mail out of there. And I would still have the same problem, it would be frozen."

— Helen Shaw, Community Member, Hague

"One of the things I have thought about is all the medication that the people get through the mail. . . . And a lot of people do their Christmas shopping—you can already see more packages. They are doing their Christmas shopping online. And there are even people who order everyday essentials online and get them in the mail."

—Lynnette Skalicky, Postmaster, McGregor

Lynnette Skalicky, Postmaster, McGregor

Tina Hanson, Postmaster Relief, McGregor

"Well, they don't have to drive as far to get to a post office; it's definitely more convenient for them."

—Tina Hanson, Postmaster Relief, McGregor

Post Office, 1st Avenue, Kathryn

"People living here would have to travel to Valley City, which is a thirty-five mile round trip, for their medications. We do get a lot of incoming packages medication-wise and not everybody lives in town or on a route."

— Sharon Coleman, Officer-in-Charge, Kathryn

Post Office, Anamoose

"They need to keep the US Postal Service going if for no other reason than to deliver medication to people. Because we've also learned . . . that those other delivery services, like UPS or FedEx, oftentimes use the US Postal Service to deliver packages the last leg. So for someplace like this, they would use the Postal Service to deliver it even though it originated with UPS."

—Brad Mincher, Community Member, Anamoose

Many rural communities in North Dakota are quite remote; they may be thirty, sixty, ninety minutes, or more from a city of more than five thousand people. This means that access to full-service grocery stores, large hardware stores, and medical centers is constrained. Consequently, mail service is a crucial link for not just specialty items but also for basic goods such as newspapers, parts and implements, clothing, and most crucial, medication. Rural residents are at a disadvantage when urban policymakers are deciding about post office closures or hour reductions and do not appreciate the centrality of the mail service in areas without local options for fulfilling basic needs.

CHAPTER 7

The Symbolic Role of the Prairie Post Office

"It's got an economic role, it's got a social role, and probably a deeper,
you know, American political role — not partisan politics but in a way of
connecting the country together, whether it's by the universality of the service
or the flag flying in front of the post office."

— Bill Anderson, Community Member, Rutland

MANY IMAGES ASSOCIATED WITH MAIL delivery have an almost iconic status: the pony express rider, the neighborhood mail carrier, the street-side blue mailboxes, and the rural letter carrier. In our interviews across rural North Dakota, the people with whom we spoke consistently alluded to such icons in an effort to convey the importance of the post office and mail delivery to their communities. The mission of the USPS is clearly and reasonably focused on mail delivery. However, as the previous chapters outlined, our interviews revealed that in rural communities the post office has acquired value and meaning beyond this original logistical intent. Indeed, these roles are especially and increasingly important as other community institutions fade away. For example, as discussed in chapter four, the multiple dimensions of the social role fulfill essential community-enhancing functions in the absence of schools, local businesses, or churches.

The last of the six roles revealed in the interviews—the symbolic role—may be the most abstract, but it plays no less an important function in community vitality. The symbolic role of the prairie post office informs beliefs about the meaning of a rural way of life, about an individual community's connection to the collective whole, about the ongoing value of tradition, and about community identity and pride.

As with areas elsewhere in the United States, rural North Dakota reflects dynamics of change and continuity. In many rural areas of North Dakota, declining populations have resulted in the loss of community institutions such as schools, churches, and businesses. In other rural areas populations have increased or held steady, with new residents gravitating to the state's economic boom, or young families and retirees moving back home or attracted to aspects of rural living. In both cases, residents discussed a rural way of life that they acknowledge can be difficult but also immensely gratifying due to the bonds between people, to their history, and to the identity that comes with being rural folk.

In our interviews, the prairie post office was referenced as representing and supporting this rural way of life. Rural postmasters, letter carriers, and other personnel are often from the community in which they work, so they know their customers. Rural postmasters assist farmers who need machinery parts delivered quickly, and postal employees contact rural residents to inform them of the safe (or sometimes not so safe!) arrival of live animals and plants. Postal employees take the time to help people find information, assist older people with carrying packages to and from their cars, and are generally part of the glue that helps hold a rural community together. A town's history and development are bound up in the history of the local post office, so for many individuals the local post office is viewed as an icon — in some cases, the last remaining icon — of the rural community.

Rural community members view the local post office as a symbol of social connectedness. Despite use of cell phones, e-mail, and other forms of electronic communication, the postal mail continues to be a source of news from distant family and friends and is also a vehicle for communicating with neighbors and acquaintances in nearby towns. Sending thank-you notes, invitations, and other pieces of hand-written mail reflect and reinforce community cohesion. But the post office also represents individual and community connection to an even larger whole. The post office building, and particularly the United States flag in front of the post office, are important indicators of the community's place in the body politic. In addition, the postmaster and other postal employees represent the federal government's attention and service to the citizenry of that locale.

The post office symbolizes for many of our interviewees a connection to the past and to the hardships and challenges overcome by ancestors and city founders. It embodies the tenacity of individuals and communities that was — and is — so much a part of contemporary rural identity. The prairie post office not only stands as a tribute to the hard work and resolve that was needed to build rural towns, but also symbolizes a kind of bridge connecting rural residents' past with their present and future.

We heard frequent references to the feelings of community loss associated with the earlier school consolidations and a concern that the same process was beginning with post office closures. This sense of loss is amplified since the post office is one of the few remaining institutions in many rural communities. Countering this sense of loss from actual or threatened post office closures, however, is a great deal of community pride. The presence of the post office — the building, its postmark, the zip code — affirms for residents that their community, as a community, is still recognized by others. For many, the symbolic connection between the post office and the community is very strong; the rural post office is a symbol of community endurance, stability, and vitality.

Kathy Aarseth, Postmaster, Fingal

"Well, I think it's kind of the heart and soul of the town. . . . we've always had it and people have always come here. And then they will run into other people and they'll visit and stuff like that. I came here as a little girl, you know, and it's just part of the town."

— Kathy Aarseth, Postmaster, Fingal

"I think the concept of the post office has been good—you know, it's just 'country crew' and people are served."

—Philip Quick, Rural Letter Carrier, Dazey

Philip Quick, Rural Letter Carrier, Dazey

Post Office, Railroad Avenue South, Leonard

"[The post office is] part of everybody's life. It's been here since Ben Franklin started it to connect people. [The loss of the post office is] going to make it harder connecting people."

—Nancy Covell, Retired Postmaster, Leonard

Linda Ehrhardt, Retired Postmaster, Almont, with husband Jim Ehrhardt and their dog Bleu

"I don't know how to put it into words. There is so much that is going [away] from our past. [The post office] helped to build our past and make it what it is. I think we need to hang onto some of the stuff. I just think we are losing it. . . . I think it's a way of life that has been passed on down."

—Linda Ehrhardt, Retired Postmaster, Almont

Former Post Office, University Avenue, Inkster

"[I]f you don't postmark it, they call it sending it in raw. I never sent mail in raw even at Christmas time when we were really busy. I always found time to stamp the mail because it just seemed to me that it was important for people, maybe even more so at that time of the year because that's the only time of the year that they keep in contact and they like to see the postmark of where it was actually coming from."

—Joanne Moreland, Retired Postmaster, Inkster

Mark Hesse, Officer-in-Charge, Tower City

"Well, if you look at all these small towns with schools that have closed, it's just another facility, it's another icon that's always been there and then if it's gone, then it's kind of a blow to your psyche or your prestige, not that this is prestigious, but it's like you're not even a town, you don't even have a post office anymore in your town."

—Mark Hesse, Officer-in-Charge, Tower City

Sherry McConnell, Postmaster, Hebron

"[The zip code is] telling you you're a town. . . . And once they lose that then usually they lose their school and then they lose the post office, and then it just starts drifting."

— Sherry McConnell, Postmaster, Hebron

"Well I think for smaller communities the post office is sort of your identity, you know, it gives your community its sense of being. . . . If you live in Cayuga, but your post office address is Lidgerwood, well which community are you then? But if your post office is there, that's your community name and that's the identity."

—Bill Anderson, Community Member, Rutland

Outside the Tower City Post Office

In its symbolic role, the prairie post office provides important meaning to residents about their community. As an institution that helped build the community and that provides services to support rural activities, the post office represents a valued and traditional way of life. The communication function of the post office, the ubiquitous flag outside the post office, and the postal employees' status as federal employees symbolize the community's connection to the larger national whole. Finally, the post office strengthens community members' sense of themselves as a community. To have a post office is to have a community identity, and the individuals we interviewed were exceedingly proud of their communities and the unique identities attached to each community. Without a post office, a community not only lost its social hub and its ability to provide convenient and vital services to community institutions and residents, but it was also on the path to losing its actual sense of self.

CHAPTER 8

Conclusion

IN 2011, THE UNITED STATES Postal Service announced the Retail Access Optimization Initiative (RAOI), which would close more than three thousand post offices across the country including seventy-six in North Dakota. Local newspapers across the state carried stories of communities organizing to resist the closure plan. The strength and passion of the resistance efforts caught our attention—it seemed clear that these communities were organizing around something more than just mail delivery. In fact, mail delivery was never in question; a larger post office in the region would take over the routes. What was and continues to be in question is the continued existence of the local post office.

After a year and ten thousand miles of visiting rural communities around the state, we did not find ghost towns. Rather we found tenacity, dedication, hospitality, and passionate articulation of the continued vitality of rural communities. We found rural residents claiming the same right to the full range of postal services as any suburban resident. We found postal employees who take great pride in the service they provide to their communities, in the unparalleled distribution network (used by commercial carriers for "last mile delivery"), and in the also unparalleled legal mandate for the sanctity and security of US mail.

Most significantly, we found that post offices and postal employees provide significant services beyond stamp sales and mail delivery. As shown in the preceding chapters, the post office serves many functions including time-honored public service, information and referral, social support, an economic catalyst, the provisioning of basic necessities, and a symbolic role.

Many people we interviewed were sympathetic to the current struggles of the USPS in light of expanding computer and internet use and changing mail use. They understood that changing demographic patterns in the nation have an impact on rural communities. Yet many also articulated a frustration with Congress for imposing extreme funding mandates on the USPS pension fund and for restricting potential avenues for service expansion in ways that would compete with private carriers like UPS and FedEx. Some even expressed the grave concern that Congress was intentionally undermining postal service in order to ease the way to privatization.

While we, the authors, understand that restructuring postal services may periodically be necessary, we believe that decisions about rural restructuring should not be guided by national ideological agendas (such as a push toward privatization) or by hasty responses to the USPS Congressional funding mandates and restrictions, especially since rural mail delivery represents a very small share of the overall USPS budget.[33] A move toward privatization of the postal service is erroneously justified under a narrow conception of efficiency and by the false belief that the private sector is inherently more efficient and effective than the public sector. Efforts at privatization in public education, the American penal system, and the US military are demonstrating neither enhanced efficiency nor effectiveness. Rural mail delivery, with its high unit costs of delivery, relative to urban areas, would be a certain loser under a privatization scheme. The US mail system has functioned as an effective public service for more than two hundred years. Its crisis occurred, not because of ineffectiveness or even inefficiency, but because in 2006 it was required to adopt an unsustainable fiscal plan.

In addition, the move to close post offices or reduce their hours across the country will inevitably hurt rural communities most, and specific populations in those communities. When the RAOI and POStPlan were announced (the first in 2011 to close more than three thousand post offices and the second in 2012 to reduce hours in more than thirteen thousand post offices), it quickly became apparent that most post office closings

and hour reductions would take place in rural areas and would most heavily impact rural poor, tribal communities, older persons, and rural businesses.[34]

Rural postal restructuring could actually serve to *support and enhance* prairie communities. People living in rural areas are often indigenous to the area or are descendants of immigrants who founded rural towns, farms, and ranches. In all cases, they have long-standing ties to the area and often hope their descendants will maintain those ties. Moreover, rural demographics wax and wane, and rural delivery responds to this fluctuation. Although the volume of first-class mail has been generally declining since 1990, the number of rural delivery points has increased 85 percent from 1990 to 2007, compared to a 12.7 percent increase over the same period for city service.[35] A single evaluative criterion like population change or mail volume fails to capture a more complicated reality.

North Dakota, with its recent oil boom, is a prime example of demographic fluctuation. Maintaining the rural postal service ensures a ready infrastructure responsive to the needs of an economic boom. But rural delivery can also support and encourage growth in rural demographics generated by those people who want to

---

[33]As the League of Postmasters pointed out in testimony before the Postal Regulatory Commission in 2011, "Indeed, if all facilities [the post offices on the RAOI list] were closed, then the maximum savings would be $200 million. That is a miniscule savings relative to the Postal Service's net deficit, as the [Center for Study of Responsible Law] points out" (National League of Postmasters, 2011, 26).

[34]"Who gets hurt when the post office closes?" (n.d.), *Save The Post Office*, http://www.savethepostoffice.com/who-gets-hurt-when-post-office-closes; M. Hoyer (August 2, 2012), "Postal cutbacks hurt rural outposts the most," USA Today, http://usatoday30.usatoday.com/news/nation/story/2012-08-01/postal-service-rural-cutbacks-post-office/56669252/1; W. LaDuke (November 11, 2011), "Rural post office closures will hurt Natives, elderly, and the poor," *The Circle: Native American News and Arts*, http://thecirclenews.org/index.php?option=com_content&task=view&id=602.

[35]United States Postal Service, "Universal Service and the Postal Monopoly: A Brief History" (October 2008), https://about.usps.com/universal-postal-service/universal-service-and-postal-monopoly-history.pdf, p. 6–7.

stay in or move to rural areas and support traditional ways of life and newer entrepreneurial efforts.

Our interviews with people across rural North Dakota have made clear that the post office in rural communities fulfills many roles essential to personal, civic, and social vitality. The mandate for the post office as stipulated in Title 39, Section 101 of the US Code and cited in the Introduction for *The Prairie Post Office* is also clear and bears repeating here:

(a) The United States Postal Service shall be operated as a basic and fundamental service provided to the people by the Government of the United States, authorized by the Constitution, created by Act of Congress, and supported by the people. The Postal Service shall have as its basic function the obligation to provide postal services to bind the Nation together through the personal, educational, literary, and business correspondence of the people. It shall provide prompt, reliable, and efficient services to patrons in all areas and shall render postal services to all communities. The costs of establishing and maintaining the Postal Service shall not be apportioned to impair the overall value of such service to the people.

(b) The Postal Service shall provide a maximum degree of effective and regular postal services to rural areas, communities, and small towns where post offices are not self-sustaining. No small post office shall be closed solely for operating at a deficit, it being the specific intent of the Congress that effective postal services be insured to residents of both urban and rural communities.

The Prairie Post Office affirms the centrality of the rural post offices and postal employees in their communities, and the federal code affirms Congressional intent to provide the same access to services to rural residents as received by urban residents. In an era of ascendant anti-government ideology and market fundamentalism, the rural post office reveals the inadequacy of such thinking. With the many challenges facing rural America, the post office emerges as an institution through which neighbors help neighbors, basic needs are delivered, social isolation is less severe, and a local economy is buoyed. Indeed, the rural post office is truly an "enlarger of the common life."

Bibliography

Hoyer, M. (August 2, 2012). "Postal cutbacks hurt rural outposts the most." *USA Today*. http://usatoday30.usatoday.com/news/nation/story/2012-08-01/postal-service-rural-cutbacks-post-office/56669252/1.

LaDuke, W. (November 11, 2011). "Rural post office closures will hurt Natives, elderly, and the poor." *The Circle. Native American News and Arts*. http://thecirclenews.org/index.php?option=com_content&task=view&id=602.

National League of Postmasters. November 10, 2011. "Reply Brief of the National League of Postmasters before the Postal Regulatory Commission re: Retail Access Optimization Initiative, Docket No. N2011-1." https://www.yumpu.com/en/document/view/25449992/reply-brief-national-league-of-postmasters/12.

United States Postal Service. "Universal Service and the Postal Monopoly: A Brief History." October 2008. https://about.usps.com/universal-postal-service/universal-service-and-postal-monopoly-history.pdf.

"Who gets hurt when the post office closes?" (n.d.). *Save The Post Office*. http://www.savethepostoffice.com/who-gets-hurt-when-post-office-closes.

Acknowledgements

IN EACH STAGE OF THIS project — research, community presentations, and book development — we were fortunate to receive the support and expertise of many individuals and organizations. The entire project, from conceptualization to book production lasted five years, and every interview, cafe lunch, back-road trek, community presentation, and research meeting was enjoyable and gratifying. North Dakota is a beautiful and fascinating state; this project further reinforced our appreciation of the land and its residents.

To support the project's research stage, we received faculty development grants from Minnesota State University Moorhead and the University of North Dakota. The North Dakota Humanities Council provided a grant for travel around the state to give presentations on our research findings, and Curt and Pam Gudmundson were kind enough to contribute funding toward the production of the book.

Mary Jo Amb, Mayville postmaster and former president of the North Dakota Chapter of the National Association of Postmasters of the United States (NAPUS), helped launch the research stage by giving us information on postal employee associations in North Dakota. Florence Oakland — retired Bisbee postmaster and previous chair, president, and vice-president of various state and national NAPUS committees — was invaluable in helping us understand some of the history and structure of the postal service in North Dakota. Florence generously agreed to fact-check our book manuscript. She was one of our interviewees and a much-appreciated cheerleader throughout the project.

Transcription is probably the most onerous task of interview research, but Jo Berg, office manager in the Department of Economics, Law, and Politics at Minnesota State University Moorhead, undertook this activity with speed and without error. We deeply appreciate her contribution to the project and her genuine interest in the stories told by interviewees.

Erik Holland, curator of education at the State Historical Society of North Dakota (SHSND), was another enthusiastic supporter of the project. Erik gave us ideas about community presentation sites and project archiving options, and he provided the opportunity to present our findings at the 2014 Governor's History Conference in Bismarck at the North Dakota Heritage Center and State Museum. The SHSND plays a vital role in supporting and preserving the cultural and historical legacies of the northern Great Plains, and we have welcomed the chance to get to know Erik and the important work of the society.

For the book's history chapter, Wayne Gudmundson recommended Kevin Carvell who, after just one phone conversation, agreed to write the text. Kevin, from Mott, North Dakota, is known for his knowledge about North Dakota history and his large personal library of books about North Dakota or by North Dakotans. Relying primarily on his own collected resources, Kevin pulled together a well-documented overview of mail delivery in northern Dakota Territory and the state of North Dakota. We are grateful to him for creating this singular contribution to North Dakota postal history.

Suzzanne Kelley, editor in chief at North Dakota State University Press, ushered the book manuscript through its many stages of development. We thank her and everyone at NDSU Press for viewing the manuscript as an important contribution to the story of North Dakota.

Friends and family were also part of this journey. Don and Sarah Lindberg, North Dakota history buffs, were regular pet-sitters when we were on the road doing interviews or presentations. Michelle Stevier listened to more than one conversation about the project and was an encouraging presence at our Medora presentation.

Jane Gudmundson hosted dinner meetings at her home and offered creative ideas for the manuscript and book design. Sam Phillips and Robert Phillips were enthusiastic supporters of the project, with Robert forwarding antique postcards of rural North Dakota towns and post offices to Amy. Dan Rice was a frequent manuscript reader and road-trip companion whose delight in the trips made them all the more enjoyable for us. We thank all of these individuals for their support and backing.

Finally, and most importantly, we thank all the individuals who agreed to be interviewed for this project. It was always surprising when a potential interviewee would answer the phone, hear an unknown voice on the other end, and after a few minutes of conversation, agree to meet two strangers who would ask questions about the role of the local post office. It shouldn't have been surprising, though, since everyone we met was welcoming (often offering coffee and even something to eat if we met at an interviewee's home) and eager to discuss her or his time with the postal service. Everyone we spoke to told eloquent, unique, and heartfelt stories related to that icon of Americana, the rural post office. We hope *The Prairie Post Office* does justice to their comments.

Appendix: North Dakota Post Offices Named on the 2011 Retail Access Optimization Initiative Closings List

POST OFFICE	ZIP CODE	POST OFFICE	ZIP CODE	POST OFFICE	ZIP CODE
Abercrombie	58001	Fort Ransom	58033	Mylo	58353
Adams	58210	Fortuna	58844	Nome	58062
Alamo	58830	Galesburg	58035	Oberon	58357
Almont	58520	Gardner	58036	Pettibone	58475
Amidon	58620	Golden Valley	58541	Robinson	58478
Antler	58711	Golva	58632	Roseglen	58775
Arnegard	58835	Grace City	58445	Rutland	58067
Baldwin	58521	Granville	58741	Saint Michael	58370
Bantry	58713	Grassy Butte	58634	Sawyer	58781
Benedict	58716	Hague	58542	Sentinel Butte	58654
Bisbee	58317	Hannaford	58448	Sharon	58277
Brocket	58321	Inkster	58244	Sheldon	58068
Buchanan	58420	Karlsruhe	58744	Spiritwood	58481
Butte	58723	Kathryn	58049	Starkweather	58377
Cartwright	58838	Kensal	58455	Tolley	58787
Clifford	58016	Kramer	58748	Tower City	58071
Cogswell	58017	Lankin	58250	Trenton	58853
Columbus	58727	Lehr	58460	Tuttle	58488
Dazey	58429	Leonard	58052	Upham	58789
Dodge	58625	Mandaree	58757	Voltaire	58792
Egeland	58331	Mantador	58058	Walcott	58077
Epping	58843	Maxbass	58760	Wildrose	58795
Erie	58029	McGregor	58755	Woodworth	58496
Fingal	58031	Mekinock	58258	Zahl	58856
Forest River	58233	Mercer	58559	Zap	58580
		Mountain	58262		

Contributors

K. Amy Phillips is a member of the Minot State University faculty and teaches social work courses in a dual degree program at North Dakota State University in Fargo. Her favorite part of North Dakota is any place that provides an expansive view of the land and sky—which is pretty much anywhere—which is why she loves living in the Flickertail State.

Steven R. Bolduc was born and raised in Massachusetts and was introduced to the Great Plains when he moved to Lincoln, Nebraska, for graduate school. Since moving to North Dakota, Steve has been captivated by the people and landscape of the northern plains. An economist by training, Steve is on the faculty of Minnesota State University Moorhead.

Wayne Gudmundson's maternal and paternal great grandparents homesteaded in North Dakota, and he has photographed the prairie landscape since 1971. His work has appeared in numerous books, exhibits, and television documentaries. Wayne recently retired from teaching photography at Minnesota State University Moorhead and now is back at work making photographs in what he calls, "that wonderful open space."

Kevin Carvell is a native of Mott, North Dakota, and a North Dakota State University graduate. After nine years at The Forum as a political reporter, he taught journalism at The University of North Dakota and then was responsible for Sen. Byron Dorgan's eastern North Dakota operations for almost a quarter century. Kevin is a student of all things North Dakota and has a personal library of some 13,000 North Dakota books.

About the Press

NORTH DAKOTA STATE UNIVERSITY PRESS (NDSU Press) exists to stimulate and coordinate interdisciplinary regional scholarship. These regions include the Red River Valley, the state of North Dakota, the plains of North America (comprising both the Great Plains of the United States and the prairies of Canada), and comparable regions of other continents. We publish peer reviewed regional scholarship shaped by national and international events and comparative studies.

Neither topic nor discipline limits the scope of NDSU Press publications. We consider manuscripts in any field of learning. We define our scope, however, by a regional focus in accord with the press's mission. Generally, works published by NDSU Press address regional life directly, as the subject of study. Such works contribute to scholarly knowledge of region (that is, discovery of new knowledge) or to public consciousness of region (that is, dissemination of information, or interpretation of regional experience). Where regions abroad are treated, either for comparison or because of ties to those North American regions of primary concern to the press, the linkages are made plain. For nearly three-quarters of a century, NDSU Press has published substantial trade books, but the line of publications is not limited to that genre. We also publish textbooks (at any level), reference books, anthologies, reprints, papers, proceedings, and monographs. The press also considers works of poetry or fiction, provided they are established regional classics or they promise to assume landmark or reference status for the region. We select biographical or autobiographical works carefully for their prospective contribution to regional knowledge and culture. All publications, in whatever genre, are of such quality and substance as to embellish the imprint of NDSU Press.

We changed our imprint to North Dakota State University Press in January 2016. Prior to that, and since 1950, we published as the North Dakota Institute for Regional Studies Press. We continue to operate under the umbrella of the North Dakota Institute for Regional Studies, located at North Dakota State University.

Index

Page numbers in **bold type** indicate photographs.